THREE INDISPENSABLE VIRTUES

Shaikh Abdul Qadir Jilani
(May Allah be pleased with him)

Tr. By: Shaikh Muhammad ibn Yahya at-Tadifi al-Hanbalion

KITAB BHAVAN
New Delhi - 110 002 (INDIA)

Name of the book : Three Indispensable Virtues

Written by : Shaikh Abdul Qadir Jilani

Translated by : Shaikh Muhammad ibn Yahya at-Tadifi al-Hanbalion

Year of Ist Edition : 2011

ISBN : 81-7151-393-X

Printed & Published by: Nusrat Ali Nasri For Kitab Bhavan

1784, Kalan Mahal, Daryaganj, New Delhi-110002

PRINTED IN INDIA

If you have any corrections, comments, or questions about this publication, please feel free to contact us.

Kitab Bhavan

1784, Kalan Mahal, Daryaganj, New Delhi-110002 (INDIA)

Phone:- (91)-11-23277392/23277393/23274686/30906494

Fax:- (91)-11-23263383, **E-Mail:-** info@kitabbhavan.com

Website:- www.kitabbhavan.com

CONTENTS

INTRODUCTION

This booklet is mainly emphasized on the vital importance of (1) repentance [tawba], (2) sincere devotion [ikhlas], and (3) the abandonment of hypocritical display [riya']. To be a good muslim and human being, it is a must for every man and woman to adopt and practice these three vital things so that his/her deeds could be accepted in the sight of Allah and he/she could get the reward in the Aakhira. Levels of sincerity (ikhlas) [in spiritual works] are three: high, medium, and low. High is for a servant to do works for Allah alone, out of obedience to His command and in fulfilment of the rights of his own slavehood. Medium is to do works seeking Allah's reward or to avoid His punishment. Low is for a servant to do works so that Allah may honour him in this world or protect him from its perils [n: e.g. praying (du'a') for such a purpose, though if it is a ***means*** to achieve something at either of the previous two levels, it takes their ruling—while all are considered sincerity (ikhlas)]. Anything besides these three is showing off (riya'). Basically the repentance is of three levels: ***tawba,*** from sins; ***tawba,*** from bad character traits; and ***inaba,*** from everything besides Allah. The Arabic term riya' is roughly translated as "showing off," which means doing something to please others or to gain their approval and admiration, instead of focusing on receiving God's approval, satisfaction, and pleasure. Riya' is the opposite of the Arabic term ikhlas [purity of intention]. According to Islam, riya' could make a pure act of worship, such as prayer, void of any reward and could even result in God's punishment. Of all the religious observances and acts of worship such as fasting [siyam] in certain months, the offering of animal sacrifice [udhiyya], the performance of ritual prayer [salat], practices of divine remembrance [adhkar], and so on, none will be accepted except after repentance [tawba], purity of heart, sincere devotion [ikhlas] to working for the sake of Allah (Exalted is He), and the abandonment of hypocritical display [riya'] and the effort to gain a reputation [sum'a].

VIRTUE OF TAWBA- REPENTANCE

1. CONCERNING THE NECESSITY OF REPENTANCE [TAWBA].

As far as repentance is concerned, in order to emphasize its importance, we shall simply add the following remarks:

Allah loves those who repent [at-tawwabin], and He loves every heart that is pure and free from sins, for He has told us (Almighty and Glorious is He):

Truly Allah loves those who turn [to Him] in repentance, and He loves those who keep themselves in purity. (2:222)
inna'llaha yuhibbu't-tawwabina wa yuhibbu'l-mutatahhirin.

'Ata', Muqatil and al-Kalbi (may Allah bestow His mercy upon them) have all told us:

"Allah loves those who turn in repentance from sins, and those who use water to purify themselves of traces of excrement [ahdath], menstrual discharge [mahid], seminal fluids [janabat], and other causes of defilement [najasat]. This is explained in the story of the people of Quba', of whom Allah (Almighty and Glorious is He) has made mention in His words (Exalted is He):

In it [in Quba'] there are men who love to purify themselves, and Allah loves those who purify themselves. (9:108)
fi-hi rijalun yuhibbuna an yatatahharu wa'llahu yuhibbu'l-muttahirin.

"The Prophet (Allah bless him and give him peace) asked them about what they did [to make themselves clean], so they told him: 'We apply water after the [rubbing with] stones in the process of istinja' [removal of impurities following acts of excretion].'"

It was Mujahid (may Allah bestow His mercy upon him) who said:

"Allah (Exalted is He) loves those who repent their sins, and those who keep themselves pure by abstaining from anal intercourse with women. If a man penetrates the anus of a women, he cannot be one of those who keep themselves pure, because the anus of a woman is similar to that of a man."

It has also been said:

"[Allah (Exalted is He) loves] those who repent their sins, and those who keep themselves pure of shirk [associating partners with Him]."

Abu'l-Minhal (may Allah bestow His mercy upon him) is reported as having said:

"On one occasion, while I was in the presence of Abu'l-'Aliya, he performed a ritual ablution [tawadda'a wudu'an] in splendid fashion, so I said to him: 'Allah loves those who turn in repentance from sins, and those who purify themselves!' To this he replied: 'Physical cleanliness is very important. Physical cleanliness is beautiful indeed, but they [the ones whom Allah loves] are those who purify themselves of sins.'"

Sa'id ibn Jubair [ibn Hisham al-Asadi] (may Allah bestow His mercy upon him) is reported as having said:

"Allah (Exalted is He) loves those who turn in repentance from shirk [associating partners with Him], and those who purify themselves of sins."

There are many other sayings on this subject, including the following:

"Allah (Exalted is He) loves those who turn in repentance from unbelief [kufr], and those who purify themselves through faith [iman]."

"Those who turn from sins in repentance do not repeat them, and those who have kept themselves pure of them have not committed them."

"Allah (Exalted is He) loves those who turn in repentance from major sins [kaba'ir], and those who keep themselves pure of minor sins [sagha'ir]."

"Allah (Exalted is He) loves those who turn in repentance from [sinful] actions [af'al], and those who keep themselves pure of [sinful] statements [aqwal]."

"Allah (Exalted is He) loves those who turn in repentance from [sinful] actions [af'al] and statements [aqwal], and those who keep themselves pure of [unlawful] contracts ['uqud] and furtive concealment [idmar]."

"Allah (Exalted is He) loves those who turn in repentance from misdeeds [atham], and those who keep themselves pure of criminal offences [ajram]."

"Allah (Exalted is He) loves those who turn in repentance from sinful deeds [jara'ir], and those who keep themselves pure of wickedness in their secret thoughts [sara'ir]."

"Allah (Exalted is He) loves those who turn in repentance from sins [dhunub], and those who keep themselves pure of faults ['uyub]."

"The penitent [tawwab] is someone who repents [taba] whenever he commits a sin."

Speaking of Himself, Allah (Almighty and Glorious is He) has told us:

He is always Forgiving to those who turn back [to Him]. (17:25)
fa-inna-hu kana li-'l-awwabina Ghafura.

According to a traditional report, transmitted by Muhammad ibn al-Munkadir on the authority of Jabir ibn 'Abdi'llah (may Allah be well pleased with him and with his father), Allah's Messenger (Allah bless him and give him peace) once said:

A man, one of those who lived before your time, once came upon a skull as he was passing by, so he looked and it and said: "Yes indeed, my Lord, You are You and I am I. You are the One who is Ever Repeating Forgiveness [Anta'l-'Awwad bi'l-maghfira], while I am the one who is ever repeating sins [ana'l-'awwad bi'dh-dhunub]." Then he fell down in humble prostration, but he was told: 'Lift up your head, for I am the One who is Ever Repeating Forgiveness [Ana'l-'Awwad bi'l-maghfira], while you are the one who is ever repeating sins [anta'l-'awwad bi'dh-dhunub].' So the man raised his head, and he was granted forgiveness.

VIRTUE OF IKHLAS
2. CONCERNING THE SIGNIFICANCE OF SINCERE DEVOTION [IKHLAS].

As for the significance of sincere devotion [ikhlas], Allah (Almighty and Glorious is He) has said:

And they have been commanded only to serve Allah, making the religion His sincerely as men of pure faith. (98:5)
wa ma umiru illa li-ya'budu'llaha mukhlisina la-hu'd-din: hunafa'a.

He has told us (Glorious and Exalted is He):

Surely pure religion is only for Allah. (39:3)
a-la li'llahi'd-dinu'l-khalis.

He has said (Exalted is He):

Their flesh and blood do not reach Allah, yet your devotion reaches Him. (22:37)
lan yanala'llaha luhumu-ha wa la dima'u-ha wa lakin yanalu-hu't-taqwa min-kum.

He has also told us (Magnificent is His Majesty):

Say [to the people of the Scripture]: "Do you dispute with us concerning Allah, when He is our Lord and your Lord?"

Ours are our works and yours are your works, and we are sincerely devoted to Him. (2:139)
qul a-tuhajjuna-na fi'llahi wa Huwa Rabbu-na wa Rabbu-kum: wa la-na a'malu-na wa la-kum a'malu-kum: wa nahnu la-hu mukhlisun.

People have held differing opinions with regard to the meaning of sincere devotion [ikhlas]. For instance, it was al-Hasan [al-Basri] (may Allah bestow His mercy upon him) who said:

"I asked Hudhaifa (may Allah be well pleased with him): 'What is meant by sincere devotion [ikhlas]?' He replied: 'I once asked the

Prophet (Allah bless him and give him peace): "What is meant by sincere devotion [ikhlas]?" He replied (Allah bless him and give him peace):

"'I once asked Gabriel (peace be upon him): "What is meant by sincere devotion [ikhlas]?" He replied: "I once asked the Lord of Might and Glory [Rabb al-'Izza] (Majestic and Exalted is He): 'What is meant by sincere devotion [ikhlas]?' So He told me (Glory be to Him and Exalted is He): 'It is a secret, a part of My secret knowledge [sirr min Sirri], which I entrust to the heart of anyone I love among My servants."

According to a report from Idris al-Khawlani (may Allah bestow His mercy upon him), Allah's Messenger (Allah bless him and give him peace) once said:

For every truth [haqq] there is a real meaning [haqiqa] to be experienced, and a servant [of the Lord] will not experience the real meaning of sincere devotion [ikhlas], until he no longer likes to be praised for any work he performs for the sake of Allah (Almighty and Glorious is He).

It was Sa'id ibn Jubair [ibn Hisham al-Asadi] (may Allah bestow His mercy upon him) who said: "The meaning of sincere devotion [ikhlas] is that the servant [of the Lord] devotes his religion sincerely to Allah, that he puts it into practice for the sake of Allah (Exalted is He), that he attributes no partner to Him in his religion, and that he does not seek to impress anyone with his religious practice."

It was al-Fudail [ibn 'Iyad at-Talaqani] (may Allah the Exalted bestow His mercy upon him) who said: "To neglect one's religious practice for the sake of other people is a form of hypocrisy [riya']. To perform one's religious practice for the sake of other people is a form of polytheistic idolatry [shirk]. As for sincere devotion [ikhlas], it is being afraid that Allah (Exalted is He) might chastise you for either of these two offences."

It was Yahya ibn Mu'adh [ar-Razi] (may Allah bestow His mercy upon him) who said: "Sincere devotion [ikhlas] means keeping one's religious practice uncontaminated by imperfections, as in the process of milking a ruminant, when the milk must be preserved from contamination by the animal's droppings and blood."

It was Abu'l-Husain al-Bushanji (may Allah bestow His mercy upon him) who said: "Sincere devotion [ikhlas] is so subtle that the two [recording] angels do not take note of it, the devil [shaitan] cannot corrupt it, and one's fellow human being is quite unaware of it."

Ruwaim (may Allah bestow His mercy upon him) once said: "Sincere devotion [ikhlas] means removing one's admiring gaze from the action performed."

Other noteworthy sayings include the following:

"Sincere devotion [ikhlas] is that which is intended to serve the truth [haqq], and which is pursued for the sake of honesty [sidq]."

"Sincere devotion [ikhlas] is that which is neither mixed with corrupting influences, nor dependent on the concessions offered by convenient interpretations [rukhas at-ta'wilat]."

"Sincere devotion [ikhlas] is that which is concealed from creatures [khala'iq] and kept free from attachments ['ala'iq]."

It was Hudhaifa al-Mar'ashi who said: "Sincere devotion [ikhlas] means that the actions of the servant [of the Lord] are of the same quality on the outside [zahir] and the inside [batin]."

It was Abu Ya'qub al-Makfuf who said: "Sincere devotion [ikhlas] means that a person keeps his good deeds hidden, just as he conceals his bad deeds."

Sahl ibn Abdi'llah [at-Tustari] once said: "Sincere devotion [ikhlas] is bankruptcy [iflas]."

According to a traditional report, transmitted on the authority of Anas ibn Malik, Allah's Messenger (Allah bless him and give him peace) once said:

There are three habits, by conforming to which the heart of a Muslim will not be invaded by rancour, malevolence, malice or spite. They are: (1) working for the sake of Allah with sincere devotion [ikhlas], (2) giving honest counsel [munasaha] to those in positions of authority, and (3) keeping closely in touch with the community [jama'a] of the Muslims.

The following anonymous sayings also deserve to be quoted:

"Sincere devotion [ikhlas] is single-minded dedication to the Truth [Haqq] in the practice of worshipful obedience [ta'a]. It means that the servant practices his worshipful obedience for the purpose of drawing near to his Master [Mawla], to the exclusion of any of His creatures. It means that he does not behave in an artificial manner, designed to impress his fellow creatures, to win their praise, to attract their love, and to shield himself against their blame and criticism."

"Sincere devotion [ikhlas] means keeping one's conduct free from the meddling influence of other creatures."

It was Dhu'n-Nun al-Misri (may Allah bestow His mercy upon him) who said: "Sincere devotion [ikhlas] does not become complete, unless it is tested by truthfulness [sidq] and practiced with patience [sabr]. Nor does truthfulness [sidq] become complete, unless it is pursued with sincere devotion [ikhlas] and practiced with constant perseverance [mudawama]."

Abu Ya'qub as-Susi had this to say on the subject: "Whenever people are sure that they can see a sincere devotion in their sincere devotion [fi ikhlasi-him ikhlasan], their 'sincere devotion' is badly in need of a dose of sincere devotion!"

Dhu'n-Nun al-Misri (may Allah bestow His mercy upon him) once said: "There are three reliable symptoms of sincere devotion [ikhlas], namely: (1) equal indifference to praise and blame from the common folk, (2) a lack of interest in the impression made by good deeds, and (3) regarding the reward for religious practice as a matter to be decided in the hereafter, [not in this world]."

He also said (may Allah bestow His mercy upon him):

"Sincere devotion [ikhlas] is that which is safe from being corrupted by the Enemy [Satan]."

It was Abu 'Uthman al-Maghribi (may Allah bestow His mercy upon him) who said: "Sincere devotion [ikhlas] is that in which the lower self [nafs] has no share whatsoever. That is the sincere devotion of the ordinary folk [ikhlas al-'awamm]. As for the sincere devotion of the elite [ikhlas al-khawass], that is something that happens to them, not because of them."

It was Abu Bakr ad-Daqqaq (may Allah bestow His mercy upon him) who said: "The shortcoming of everyone who tries to be sincere [mukhlis] in his sincere devotion, is the tendency to admire his sincere devotion [ikhlas]. If Allah (Exalted is He) wishes to purify his sincere devotion [an yukhallisa ikhlasa-hu], He will therefore rid his sincerity of that tendency to admire his sincere devotion, so he will then be a mukhallas [one who has been made sincere through purification], rather than a mukhlis [one who tries to be sincere]."

Sahl [ibn Abdi'llah at-Tustari] (may Allah bestow His mercy upon him) once said: "No one can see through hypocritical display [riya'], apart from one who is sincere [mukhlis]."

It was Abu Sa'id al-Kharraz (may Allah bestow His mercy upon him) who said: "The pretentiousness of those who know by direct experience [riya' al-'arifin] is worth more than the sincere devotion of the novices [ikhlas al-muridin]."

Abu 'Uthman [al-Maghribi] (may Allah bestow His mercy upon him) also said: "Sincere devotion [ikhlas] means forgetting to notice one's fellow creatures [khalq], through paying constant attention to the Creator [Khaliq]."

One of the wise once said:

"Sincere devotion [ikhlas] is that by which the truth [haqq] is sought, and which is pursued for the sake of honesty [sidq]."

It was Sari as-Saqati (may Allah bestow His mercy upon him) who said: "If someone tries to impress other people, by flaunting something he does not have within him, he will fall from grace in the sight of Allah (Exalted is He)."

It was al-Junaid (may Allah bestow His mercy upon him) who said: "Sincere devotion [ikhlas] is a secret between Allah (Exalted is He) and the servant [of the Lord]. No angel is privy to it, to be able to record it, nor any devil [shaitan], to be able to corrupt it, and no passionate desire, to be able to distort it."

Ruwaim (may Allah bestow His mercy upon him) once said: "Sincere devotion [ikhlas], in religious work, is that for which its practitioner seeks no recompense in either of the two Abodes [ad-Darain], nor any share in the two Domains [al-Mulkain]."

When someone asked [Sahl] ibn 'Abdi'llah [at-Tustari] (may Allah bestow His mercy upon him): "What is the hardest thing for the lower self [nafs] to bear?" he replied: "Sincere devotion [ikhlas], because it has no share therein."

To quote another anonymous saying: "Sincere devotion [ikhlas] means that you invite no one, apart from Allah (Almighty and Glorious is He) to notice your religious practice."

The following incidents were reported by one of the righteous, who said:

"I paid a visit to Sahl ibn 'Abdi'llah [at-Tustari] (may Allah bestow His mercy upon him), one Friday before the congregational prayer [salat]. I spotted a snake in the house, so I started taking one step forward and another step back, but he said: 'Come on in! No one attains to the reality of faith [haqiqat al-iman], as long as there is anything, on the face of the earth, of which he is still afraid.' Then he went on to say: 'Are you thinking of attending the congregational prayer [salat al-jum'a]?' 'Hardly,' said I, 'since it would take a day and a night to travel the distance between here and the mosque [masjid].' So he took me by the hand, and it seemed like no time at all before I could see the mosque. We went inside and performed the congregational prayer [sallaina'l-jum'a], then we came outside again. Sahl stood and watched the people as they emerged, then he said: 'Many are those who repeat the words: "There is no god but Allah [la ilaha illa'llah]," but few of them are sincere [mukhlisin].'"

"On another occasion, when I was with Ibrahim al-Khawwas (may Allah bestow His mercy upon him) on a journey, we came to a place in which there were many snakes. He laid his water-flask [rakwa] on the ground, and sat down, so I sat down too. Then, when the night turned cool, and the air grew cold, out came the snakes. I yelled at the Shaikh in alarm, but he said: 'Just remember Allah (Exalted is He),' so I remembered Him, and the snakes recoiled. But then they came back again, so I yelled at the Shaikh, and he gave me the same advice as before. I found myself in that same situation, right through to the break of day. Then, when the dawn had arrived, he stood up and started walking, so I walked along with him. Suddenly, out of the seat of his pants, there fell a huge serpent, which had gathered itself into a coil. 'Did you not feel it?' I asked, but he said: 'No, it has been a long time since I spent a night as pleasant as this last one.'"

It was Abu 'Uthman [al-Maghribi] (may Allah the Exalted bestow His mercy upon him) who said: "If a person has never tasted the lonely isolation of heedlessness [wahsat al-ghafla], he will never discover the sweet taste of the intimate friendship of remembrance [uns adh-dhikr]."

VIRTUE OF ABANDONMENT OF RIYA
3. CONCERNING THE NECESSITY TO BE CONSTANTLY ON GUARD AGAINST HYPOCRITICAL DISPLAY [RIYA'], THE DESIRE TO IMPRESS ONE'S FELLOW CREATURES [RU'YAT AL-KHALQ], AND VAIN CONCEIT ['UJB].

It is most important for every devout worshipper [muta'abbid] and truly experienced believer ['arif] to be constantly on guard, in all his conditions and circumstances, against hypocritical display [riya'], the desire to impress his fellow creatures [ru'yat al-khalq], and vain conceit ['ujb]. This is because the lower self [nafs] is maligned. It is the source of misleading desires, pernicious appetites, and lustful passions that form a barrier between the servant and the Lord of Truth (Almighty and Glorious is He). There is no road to safety from its wicked and mischievous ways, as long as the spirit [ruh] resides within the body of a human being [ibn Adam].

This is still the case, even if the servant [of the Lord] attains to the state of Spiritual Deputyship [Badaliyya] and Championship of the Truth [Siddiqiyya], although this state is safer than the initial stage of spiritual development, and more secure from the wickedness and the cunning wiles of the lower self [nafs]. In this state, the good is more predominant, the light is more prevalent, the guidance is positively in the direction of Allah's path [fi sabili'llah], the enabling grace [tawfiq] is comprehensive, and the needed protection is always available. Impeccable virtue ['isma] is not for us, however. That is a quality peculiar to the Prophets [Anbiya'] (peace be upon them all), conferred on them in order to draw the distinction between Prophetship [Nubuwwa] and saintship [wilaya].

Allah (Almighty and Glorious is He) has issued a warning threat to those who practice hypocritical display [riya'] and seek to promote an undeserved reputation [sum'a]. He has cautioned us against the wicked inclination of the lower self [nafs] and its mischievous tricks. He has forbidden us to follow its dictates, and He has instructed us to oppose and contradict it, sometimes in the Qur'an, and at other times in the utterances of Allah's Messenger (Allah bless him and give him peace), which are recorded in the traditional reports [akhbar] and enshrined in the Sunna. Let us first consider some examples from the Qur'an [and other Scriptures]:

Allah (Almighty and Glorious is He) has said:

So woe to those who pray, but are heedless of their prayers, and to those who make a show, yet withhold the smallest charity. (107:4,5)
fa-wailun li'l-musallin: alladhina hum 'an salati-him sahun: alladhina hum yura'una wa yamna'una'l-ma'un.

He has said (Glorious and Exalted is He):

They utter with their mouths what is not in their hearts Allah is best aware of what they hide. (3:167)
yaquluna bi-afwahi-him ma laisa fi qulubi-him: wa'llahu a'lamu bi-ma yaktumun.

He has said (Exalted is He):

The hypocrites seek to beguile Allah but it is He who beguiles them. When they stand up to perform the prayer, they perform it languidly and to impress people, and they are mindful of Allah but little.
inna'l-munafiqina yukhadi'una'llaha wa Huwa khadi'u-hum: wa idha qamu ila 's-salati qamu kasala yura'una'n-nasa wa la yadhkuruna'llaha illa qalila.

[They are] swaying between this [and that], belonging neither to these nor to those. If Allah causes someone to go astray, you will not find a way for him. (4:142,143)
mudhabdhabina baina dhalik: la ila ha'ula'i wa la ila ha'ula':
wa man yudlili'llahu fa-lan tajida la-hu sabila.

He has said (Exalted is He):

O you who believe, many of the [Jewish] rabbis and the [Christian] monks devour the wealth of mankind wantonly, and debar [men] from the way of Allah. (9:34) ya ayyuha'lladhina amanu inna kathiran mina'l-ahbari wa'r-ruhbani la-ya'kuluna amwala'n-nasi bi-'l-batili wa yasudduna 'an sabili'llah.

He has said (Almighty and Glorious is He):

O you who believe, why do you say that which you do not do? It is most hateful in the sight of Allah that you say what you do not do. (61:2)
ya ayyuha'lladhina amanu li-ma taquluna ma la taf'alun: kabura maqtan 'inda'llahi an taqulu ma la taf'alun.

He has said (Exalted is He):

Keep your words private or speak openly; He knows what the breasts contain. (67:13)
wa asirru qawla-kum awi 'jharu bi-h:inna-hu 'Alimun bi-dhati's-sudur.

He has said (Glorious and Exalted is He):

So whoever hopes for the meeting with his Lord, let him do righteous work, and let him give no one any share at all in the worship due unto his Lord. (18:110)
fa-man kana yarju liqa'a Rabbi-hi fa-'l-ya'mal 'amalan salihan wa la yushrik bi-'ibadati Rabbi-hi ahada.

He has said (Exalted is He): Surely the self is always inciting to evil, except inasmuch as my Lord has mercy. (12:53)
inna'n-nafsa la-ammaratun bi's-su'i illa ma rahima Rabbi.

He has said (Exalted is He):

But greed has been made present in the souls [of men]. (4:128)
wa uhdirati'l-anfusu'sh-shuhh.

He said (Almighty and Glorious is He) to David [Dawud] (peace be upon him) [in a non-Qur'anic utterance]:

O David, you must flee from your passionate desire [hawa], for no contender challenges Me for My dominion, apart from passionate desire.

He has also said (Exalted is He):

Do not follow passionate desire, lest it lead you astray from Allah's path. (38:26)
wa la tattabi'i'l-hawa fa-yudilla-ka 'an sabili'llah.

As for the Sunna, Shaddad ibn Aws (may Allah be well pleased with him) is reported as having said: "I once entered the presence of the Prophet (Allah bless him and give him peace), and I noticed a look in his face that made me shudder, so I said: 'What is the matter with you, O Messenger of Allah?' He replied (Allah bless him and give him peace):

"'I am afraid that my Community [Ummati] may be guilty of shirk [attributing partners to Allah], after I am gone.'"

"On hearing this, I exclaimed: 'Do you really mean to say, O Messenger of Allah, that they will attribute partners to Him [yushrikuna] after you are gone?' So he went on to explain (Allah bless him and give him peace):

"'They may not worship a sun, or a moon, or a graven image [wathan], or a stone idol, but they will resort to hypocritical display in their religious practices [a'mal], and hypocritical display [riya'] is tantamount to shirk [attributing partners to Allah].'"

"Then he recited the words of Allah (Exalted is He):

So whoever hopes for the meeting with his Lord, let him do righteous work, and let him give no one any share at all in the worship due unto his Lord. (18:110)"
fa-man kana yarju liqa'a Rabbi-hi fa-'l-ya'mal 'amalan salihan wa la yushrik bi-'ibadati Rabbi-hi ahada.

The Prophet (Allah bless him and give him peace) once said:

The Day of Resurrection [Yawm al-Qiyama] will come with sealed scrolls [suhuf makhtuma] [in which the deeds of mankind have been recorded], so Allah (Almighty and Glorious is He) will say to the angels:

"Throw this one away, and accept this one." They will respond by saying: "By Your Might and Your Majesty, we know nothing but good." So He will say (Exalted is He): "Yes, but this is [the record of] a deed performed for someone other than Me, and I only accept what was done for the sake of My countenance."

The Prophet (Allah bless him and give him peace) used to say, in his prayer of supplication [du'a']:

O Allah, make my tongue pure and free from lying, my heart from hypocrisy [nifaq], my religious practice from hypocritical display [riya'], and my eyesight from treachery, for You know the treachery of the eyes, and what the breasts conceal.

He once said (Allah bless him and give him peace):

You must not sit at the feet of a religious scholar ['alim], unless he summons you away from five toward five, namely: (1) away from indulgence [raghba], in the direction of abstinence [zuhd]; (2) away from hypocritical display [riya'], in the direction of sincere devotion [ikhlas]; (3) away from arrogant pride [kibr], in the direction of modest humility [tawadu']; (4) away from fawning flattery [mudahana], in the direction of honest advice [munasaha]; and (5) away from ignorance [jahl], in the direction of knowledge ['ilm].

He once said (Allah bless him and give him peace):

Allah (Exalted is He) says: "I am the Best Partner [Ana Khairu Sharik]. If someone associates a partner with Me, in his undertaking, it involves the partner ascribed to Me [shariki] and has nothing to do with Me. I accept only that which is devoted solely to Me. O Children of Adam, I am the Best Participant [Ana Khairu Qasim], so reconsider that work of yours, which you have performed for someone other than Me, because your wage is incumbent only on the one for whom you did the work."

He also said (Allah bless him and give him peace):

You may congratulate this Community [Umma] on their brilliance and high standing in the sphere of religion, and on their empowerment in the countries of the earth, so long as they do not perform the work of the hereafter for the sake of this world. If anyone does the work of the hereafter for the sake of this world, it will not be accepted of him, and in the hereafter he will have no share.

He also said (Allah bless him and give him peace):

Allah will surely grant the benefits of this world [for work performed] with the intention of gaining the benefits of the hereafter, but He will not grant the benefits of the hereafter [for work performed] with the intention of gaining the benefits of this world.

As reported on the authority of Anas ibn Malik (may Allah be well pleased with him), Allah's Messenger (Allah bless him and give him peace) once said:

On the night when I was taken on my Heavenly Journey [usriya bi], I passed by a group of people whose lips had been snipped by scissors of fire. "Who are these?" I said to Gabriel (peace be upon him), so he told me: "They are the preachers [khutaba'] of your Community. They say something, but they do not put it into practice. They say what they acknowledge as being correct, but they do what they denounce as being wrong. They instruct the people to act righteously, but they forget to include themselves.

He also said (Allah bless him and give him peace):

The worst of my fears for my Community [Ummati] is every hypocrite [munafiq] with a clever tongue. By the One who holds my soul in His hand, the Final Hour will not come about until they find themselves subject to dishonest rulers, immoral ministers, treacherous assistants, iniquitous professors ['urafa'], dissolute Qur'an-reciters [qurra'], and ignorant servants. Allah (Exalted is He) will expose them to dark and murky intrigue, so they will experience a bewildering perplexity [tahawwuk], like that which afflicted the wrong-doing Jews [Yahud]. From that point on, Islam will unravel, knot by knot, until no one says: "Allah, Allah!"

As reported on the authority of 'Adi ibn Hatim (may Allah be well pleased with him), Allah's Messenger (Allah bless him and give him peace) once said:

On the Day of Resurrection [Yawm al-Qiyama], certain people will be subjected to exemplary punishment of the most extreme kind. Allah (Exalted is He) will say to them: "When you were in private situations, you would brazenly affront Me with heinous sins ['aza'im], but when you met with other people, you would approach them modestly and humbly. You were in awe of other people, but you did not regard Me with awe. You honoured other people, but you did not honour Me. By My Might, I shall make you taste the most painful chastisement."

According to a traditional report, Usama ibn Zaid (may Allah be well pleased with him and with his father) once heard Allah's Messenger (Allah bless him and give him peace) say:

A man will be cast into the Fire of Hell, so his guts will soon be dangling out of his belly. He will be rotated as a mill is rotated by its owner, and he will be asked: "Were you not in the habit of enjoining that which is right and fair [ma'ruf], and forbidding that which is wrong and unfair [munkar]?" To this he will reply: "I used to enjoin what is right and fair [ma'ruf], though I did not practice it myself, and I used to forbid is wrong and unfair [munkar], though I did not abstain from it myself."

The Prophet (Allah bless him and give him peace) once said:

Many a keeper of the fast [sa'im] receives nothing from his fasting [siyam] but hunger and thirst, and many a keeper of night vigil [qa'im] receives nothing from his vigil [qiyam] but insomnia.

To this the Prophet (Allah bless him and give him peace) added:

The Heavenly Throne ['Arsh] trembles because of that, and the Lord (Blessed and Exalted is He) is angry with him.

The Prophet (Allah bless him and give him peace) once said:

What a bad servant [of the Lord] is a servant who erects a barrier between himself and the spiritual reward of Allah (Exalted is He)! I am speaking of a servant, one of the creatures of Allah (Exalted is He), who devotes himself to His service, in the hope of receiving what He has at His disposal, and who exhausts his physical body in the effort to obtain His approval, but who makes a public show of his religious devotion [din], which is thereby rendered invalid.

His manly virtue [muru'a] degenerates into vice, and so he erects a barrier between himself and his Lord. He pins his hopes on Allah (Exalted is He), as far as the big picture is concerned, but he pins them on his fellow servant, when it comes to the small details. He gives some of his service to his fellow servant, at the expense of his worshipful obedience [ta'a] to Allah (Exalted is He).

Mujahid (may Allah bestow His mercy upon him) is reported as having said: "A man once came to Allah's Messenger (Allah bless him and give him peace) and said: 'O Messenger of Allah, I make it my practice to give charitable donations [atasaddaqu bi-sadaqa], so that I may obtain the gracious favour of Allah (Exalted is He). I also like to hear people speaking well of me.' At that very moment, His words (Blessed and Exalted is He):

So whoever hopes for the meeting with his Lord, let him do righteous work, and let him give no one any share at all in the worship due unto his Lord. (18:110) fa-man kana yarju liqa'a Rabbi-hi fa-'l-ya'mal 'amalan salihan wa la yushrik bi-'ibadati Rabbi-hi ahada.

--were sent down [to the Prophet (Allah bless him and give him peace)]."

The Prophet (Allah bless him and give him peace) once said:

The end of the age will see the emergence of groups of people who exploit religion [din] for worldly purposes. To impress other people, they will dress in sheep's clothing, and their tongues will be sweeter than sugar, though their hearts are the hearts of wolves. Allah (Exalted is He) will say: "Are you deluding yourselves about Me, or are you so bold as to challenge Me deliberately?" I swear by Me, I shall surely inflict such confusion upon those people, that you would call the mildest case a case of utter bewilderment."

As we learn from a traditional report, Allah's Messenger (Allah bless him and give him peace) once said:

The angels will carry aloft the work of a certain servant from among the servants of Allah. They will multiply it and purify it, until they finally bring it to wherever Allah (Exalted is He) wishes it to be delivered, in all of His Dominion [Sultan]. Allah will thereupon convey to them, by way of inspiration: "You are custodians of My servant's work, while I am Ever-Watchful [Raqib] over what is in his soul [nafs]. This servant of Mine has not devoted his work sincerely to Me, so register him in the Deepest Pit [Sijjin]."

They will also rise aloft with the work of another servant from among His servants. They will diminish it and belittle it, until they finally bring it to wherever Allah (Exalted is He) wishes it to be delivered, in all of His Dominion [Sultan]. Allah will thereupon convey to them, by way of inspiration: "You are custodians of My servant's work, while I am Ever-Watchful [Raqib] over what is in his soul [nafs]. This servant of Mine has devoted his work sincerely to Me [akhlasa li 'amala-hu], so register him in the Highest Heaven ['Iliyyin]."

As reported on the authority of Abu Huraira (may Allah be well pleased with him), Allah's Messenger (Allah bless him and give him peace) once said:

On the Day of Resurrection [Yawm al-Qiyama], Allah (Blessed and Exalted is He) will judge between His creatures, while the members of every religious community [umma] fall on their knees. The first to be summoned will be a man who compiled a copy of the Qur'an, a man who was slain while fighting for Allah's cause [fi sabili'llah], and a man who possessed considerable wealth.

To the expert on the Qur'an [qari'], Allah (Exalted is He) will then say: "To what extent did you put what you learned into practice?" The man will reply: "I used to act upon it through the watches of the night, and at all times during the day." But Allah (Blessed and Exalted is He) will say: "You have told a lie!" The angels will also say: "You have told a lie! What you wanted, in fact, was to have people call you 'Qur'an-expert so and so,' and you did indeed acquire that title."

The owner of wealth will be asked: "What did you do, to make good use of all that I made available to you?" The man will reply: "I was the source of compassion, and I applied it to charitable purposes." But Allah (Blessed and Exalted is He) will say: "You have told a lie!" The angels will also say: "You have told a lie! What you wanted, in fact, was to have people call you 'Generous Mister So-and-so,' and that was indeed how you came to be called."

The man who was slain while fighting for the cause of Allah (Exalted is He) will also be brought forward. To him Allah (Exalted is He) will say: "For what did you do battle?" The man will reply: "I fought for Your cause, until I was slain in Your cause." But Allah (Blessed and Exalted is He) will say: "You have told a lie!" The angels will also say: "You have told a lie! What you wanted, in fact, was to have people call you 'Brave Hero So-and-so,' and that was indeed how you came to be called."

At this point, Allah's Messenger (Allah bless him and give him peace) thumped his hands on his knees, and said:

"O Abu Huraira, on the Day of Resurrection [Yawm al-Qiyama], those three will be the first of the creatures of Allah (Almighty and Glorious is He) to be scorched by the Fire of Hell!"

Abu Huraira (may Allah be well pleased with him) also said: This report came to the attention of Mu'awiya (may Allah be well pleased with him). On hearing it, he experienced an intense bout of weeping, then he said: 'Allah (Exalted is He) has spoken the truth, and His Messenger (Allah bless him and give him peace) has spoken the truth.' Then he recited these Qur'anic verses [ayat]:

As for those who desire the life of this world and its pomp, We shall repay them for their deeds therein, and therein they will not be wronged.
man kana yuridu'l-hayata'd-dunya wa zinata-ha nuwaffi ilai-him a'mala-hum fi-ha wa hum fi-ha la yubkhasun.

Such are those for whom there is nothing in the Hereafter but the Fire. All that they contrive here is vain, and all that they are used to doing is fruitless. (11:15,16)
ula'ika'lladhina laisa la-hum fi'l-akhirati illa'n-nar: wa habita ma sana'u fi-ha wa batilun ma kanu ya'malun.

Such are those for whom is the worst of torment, and in the Hereafter they will be among the greatest losers. (27:5)
ula'ika'lladhina la-hum su'u'l-'adhabi wa hum fi'l-akhirati humu'l-akhsarun.

According to another traditional report, transmitted on the authority of 'Adi ibn Hatim at-Ta'i (may Allah be well pleased with him), Allah's Messenger (Allah bless him and give him peace) once said:

On the Day of Resurrection [Yawm al-Qiyama], the order will be given for some of those destined for the Fire of Hell to be herded toward the Garden of Paradise. They will be allowed to get close enough to smell its fragrant perfume, to view its palatial mansions, and to see what Allah (Exalted is He) has prepared for its inhabitants. Then they will hear the call: "Take them away! In this they have no share." So they will return whence they came, with a sense of distress and remorse, the like of which was never experienced by anyone making a return journey, in ancient or later times. They will say: "O our Lord, if only You had caused us to enter the Fire of Hell directly, before showing us what You have just shown us, meaning the reward You have prepared for those others!"

Allah (Exalted is He) will then say: "That is how I saw fit to treat you. When you were in private situations, you would brazenly affront Me with heinous sins ['aza'im], but when you met with other people, you would approach them modestly and humbly. By making a show of your deeds, you would give people an impression contrary to what was hidden away in your hearts. You were in awe of other people, but you did not regard Me with awe. You honoured other people, but you did not honour Me. You abstained, to please other people, from things you did not abandon for My sake. Today, therefore, I am giving you a taste of My painful chastisement, combined with a glimpse of My abundant reward, of which you have been deprived."

As reported on the authority of Ibn 'Abbas (may Allah be well pleased with him and with his father), Allah's Messenger (Allah bless him and give him peace) once said:

When Allah (Exalted is He) created the Garden of Eden [Jannat 'Adn], He created within it that which no eye has ever seen, of which no ear has ever heard, and the very notion of which has never occurred to the human heart. Then He said to it: "Speak to Me," and it responded by saying three times:

Successful indeed are the true believers. (23:1)
qad aflaha'l-mu'minun.

Then the Garden went on to say: "I am forbidden [haram] to every miser [bakhil] and ostentatious hypocrite [mura'i]."

A man once asked Allah's Messenger (Allah bless him and give him peace): "In what does salvation reside, tomorrow [at the Resurrection]?" He replied:

You must not try to deceive Allah (Exalted is He).

The man then asked: "How could I be guilty of trying to deceive Allah (Almighty and Glorious is He)?" The Prophet (Allah bless him and give him peace) explained:

By doing what He has commanded you to do, but doing it for some purpose other than to obtain the gracious favour of Allah (Exalted is He).

All of you must therefore beware of hypocritical display [riya'], for it is tantamount to associating partners [shirk] with Allah (Exalted is He). Indeed, on the Day of Resurrection [Yawm al-Qiyama], the ostentatious hyprocrite [mura'i] will be summoned by four names, over the heads of all the assembled creatures: "O unbeliever [ya kafir]! O shameless liar [ya fajir]! O traitor [ya ghadir]! O loser [ya khasir]! Your work has gone astray, and your recompense has been cancelled, so there is no share for you here today. Apply for your wages to those for whom you used to work, O deceiver!" Let us therefore take refuge with Allah (Almighty and Glorious is He) from hypocritical display [riya'], from promoting an undeserved reputation [sum'a], and from hypocrisy itself [nifaq], for that is the work of those who are doomed to the Fire of Hell.

Allah (Almighty and Glorious is He) has said:

Surely the hypocrites will be in the lowest depth of the Fire [of Hell]. (4:145)
inna'l-munafiqina fi'd-darki'l-asfali mina'n-nar.

In other words, they will be in the Pit [al-Hawiya], in the company of Pharaoh [Fir'awn] and Haman and their people.

As someone might well see fit to interject at this point, it seems be suggested, in at least one of the traditional reports [akhbar], that there is actually no harm in having our religious practice noticed by our fellow creatures. According to the report in question, it was Abu Huraira (may Allah be well pleased with him) who said:

"A man came to Allah's Messenger (Allah bless him and give him peace) and said: 'O Messenger of Allah, I perform my religious practice, intending to keep it private, but I find that people are watching, and that pleases me. If such be the case, am I entitled to any reward?' To this he replied (Allah bless him and give him peace):

'You are entitled to two rewards: the reward for the secrecy, and the reward for the publicity.'"

To resolve what may appear to be a contradiction, this should be construed as follows: What made that man feel pleased, was the fact that people followed the example he was setting, in the performance of his religious practice. Allah's Messenger (Allah bless him and give him peace) was aware of this, so he told the man, in effect: "You are entitled to two rewards: one reward for your righteous work, and one reward for having people follow your good example." As he once said (Allah bless him and give him peace):

If someone establishes a good custom [sanna sunnatan hasana], he is entitled to the reward for it, and also to the reward of all those who practice it, until the Day of Resurrection [Yawm al-Qiyama]....

On the other hand, if someone enjoys the pleasing sensation in and of itself, and not on account of the good example he is setting for others, he is not entitled to any reward, because vain conceit ['ujb] can only cause the servant to fall from grace in the sight of Allah.

It was al-Hasan al-Basri (may Allah bestow His mercy upon him) who said: "If you wish, you may choose a companion with a fair complexion, but with crude manners, one who has a smooth tongue and a sharp eye, but who is dead at heart. You see physical bodies, not hearts. You listen to the sound of music, but not to a close friend. Tongues have grown fertile, while hearts have turned barren.

"As a matter of fact, several Companions [Ashab] of Allah's Messenger (Allah bless him and give him peace) have told me that this Community [Umma] will remain beneath the hand of Allah, in His protective custody, but only as long as its Qur'an-reciters [qurra'] and its commanders [umara'] do not lose interest in their work, as long as its honest members [sulaha'] do not join the ranks of the lying scoundrels [fujjar], and as long as its best representatives keep the worst at bay. As soon as they reverse their positions, Allah (Exalted is He) will remove His protecting hand from them. He will smite them with poverty and want. He will fill their hearts with terror, and He will subject them to the rule of tyrants [jababira], who will make them suffer dreadful torment."

He [al-Hasan al-Basri (may Allah bestow His mercy upon him)] also said: "What a bad servant [of the Lord] is he! I am speaking of a servant who fits the following description:

He asks for forgiveness [maghfira], while he is actively engaged in sinful disobedience [ma'siya].

He behaves in a humbly submissive manner, so that he may be credited with loyalty [amana], but he is only pretending, to hide his disloyalty [khiyana].

He forbids what is wrong, but does not refrain from it himself [yanha wa la yantahi].

He enjoins what is right, but does not act upon his own instructions.

If he gives, he does so very stingily, and if he withholds, he offers no apology.

If he is in the best of health, he feels secure, but if he falls sick, he becomes remorseful.

If he is impoverished, he feels sad, and if he gets rich, he is subject to temptation.

He hopes for salvation, but does not act accordingly.

He is afraid of punishment, but takes no precautions against it.

He wishes to receive more benefit, but he does not give thanks [for what he has received].

He likes the idea of spiritual reward, but he does not practice patience.

He expedites sleep [nawm], and postpones fasting [sawm]."

He [al-Hasan al-Basri (may Allah bestow His mercy upon him)] spoke one day to Farqad as-Sabakhi, who was sitting in attendance at his meeting [majlis]. In sharp contrast to al-Hasan, who was dressed in very smart attire, Farqad was wearing a jubba made of wool [suf]. "My clothing," said al-Hasan, "is the clothing of the people of the Garden of Paradise, while your clothing is the clothing of the people of the Fire of Hell. They lodge their pious abstinence [zuhd] in their clothing, and their arrogant pride in their breasts. By Allah, any one of them is far more conceited about his wool [suf] than a fashionable shawl-designer is about his fancy shawl. What is wrong with competing together in excellence? Why not dress outwardly in the style of kings, and kill your hearts with fear [of displeasing the Lord]?"

'Umar [ibn al-Khattab] (may Allah be well pleased with him) once said: "You should dress in a style that will neither cause the Qur'an-reciters [qurra'] to treat you as a laughing-stock, nor make silly idiots deride you."

As they used to say: "Be woollen [sufi] at heart, and cotton-made [qutni] in clothing."

To put the subject in a nutshell, the people [who matter to us] fall into three categories, where clothing is concerned: (1) the devout [atqiya'], (2) the saints [awliya'], and (3) the spiritual deputies [abdal].

The clothing of the devout [atqiya'] is that which is lawful [halal], in the sense that none of the wearer's fellow creatures have any claim on it, and that it does not violate the sacred law [shar'] in any respect. As for whether their clothes are of cotton [qutn] or wool [suf], and whether they are white or blue, that is neither here not there.

The clothing of the saints [awliya'] is determined by the [divine] commandment. At the very least, it must be sufficient to cover the genital area ['awra], and any other part of the body for which it is essential. Some form of clothing is called for, of necessity, to ensure the discouragement of their passionate desires, so that they may attain to the degree of the spiritual deputies [abdal].

The clothing of the spiritual deputies [budala'] is whatever destiny [qadar] brings to the individual concerned, always with due respect to the limits set by the sacred law [hudud]. It may be a plain shirt worth a mere qirat [one twentieth of a dinar], or a fine suit worth a hundred dinars [gold coins], for there is no self-will involved. They have ascended to the highest height, and there is no passionate desire to be discouraged at the lowest level. For them, it is simply a matter of accepting whatever the Master [Mawla] graciously confers, whatever He allows and bestows, without trouble or concern, and without respect for the lower self [nafs] and personal preferences.

Aside from these perspectives, any other approach to the subject can be traced to the ancient Time of Ignorance [Jahiliyya], to the frivolous inclination of the lower self [nafs], and to the influence of passionate desire [hawa].